WHEELS OF TIME

A BIOGRAPHY

OF HENRY FORD

WHEELS OF TIME

A BIOGRAPHY

OF HENRY FORD

BY CATHERINE GOURLEY

IN ASSOCIATION WITH
HENRY FORD MUSEUM
& GREENFIELD VILLAGE
DEARBORN, MICHIGAN

THE MILLBROOK PRESS
Brookfield, Connecticut

Published by The Millbrook Press, Inc.
2 Old New Milford Road, Brookfield, Connecticut 06804
Text copyright © 1997 by Catherine Gourley
Photograph on page 13 © Sandra Eisner/Photonica
All other photographs are from the collections of Henry Ford Museum & Greenfield Village

Printed in the United States of America
5 4 3 2 1

Book Design by Tania Garcia
Text is set in 14 pt. Centaur

Library of Congress Cataloging-in-Publication Data
Gourley, Catherine, 1950–
Wheels of time : a biography of Henry Ford / by Catherine Gourley.
p.   cm.
"Published in association with Henry Ford Museum & Greenfield Village."
Summary: A biography of the engineer and industrialist whose innovative methods enabled his company to build and mass-produce reliable and inexpensive automobiles and whose later years were
devoted to establishing a museum reflecting American life before the advent of machines.
ISBN 0-7613-0214-X
1. Ford, Henry, 1863–1947—Juvenile literature.
2. Industrialists—United States—Biography—Juvenile literature. 3. Automobile industry and
trade—United States—Biography—Juvenile literature.
[1. Ford, Henry, 1863–1947. 2. Industrialists. 3. Automobile industry and trade—Biography.]
I. Henry Ford Museum & Greenfield Village. II. Title.
TL140.F6G68 1997
338.7'6292'092—dc21
[B] 97-3616 CIP AC

WHEELS OF TIME

The air is full of ideas. They are knocking you on the head. You don't have to think about it too much. You only have to know what you want.

— Henry Ford

As a child, Henry Ford knew what he wanted. He wanted to look inside things, to take things apart to see how they worked, and then to put them back together again.

Each Saturday during the family's shopping trip to Detroit, Henry sneaked away to the riverfront. Boats with giant paddle wheels churned the water. He wandered along the docks past warehouses and mills. Inside were saws that whined and drills that sparked as they bit into wood and metal. Pulleys with leather belts slapped as they spun round and round. In Detroit in the 1860s and 1870s, the air was full of power and movement and ideas. And the main idea was this: Machines were building the future.

Henry Ford knew what he wanted. He wanted to become a mechanic and build the future, too.

PART I:
MARBLES FOR CLOCK WHEELS

Machines are to a mechanic what books are to a writer. He gets _____ *hem, and if he has any brains, he applies those ideas.*

_____y Ford

Henr_____ bedroom of a small farmhouse in _____ on July 30, 1863. He was the
oldest son of _____ Mary Litogot Ford.

Henry's natural curiosity _____ e been sparked by an early childhood
experience. When he was four ye_____ old, his father and mother took Henry
and his younger brother John into a pasture to spy on the nest of a song

Left: Henry Ford's birthplace
Above: Henry Ford, age 2½

Left: *Henry's father, William Ford*

Right: *Henry's mother, Mary Litogot Ford*

sparrow. William held John in his arms. Mary lifted Henry onto a log so he could see, too. Cupped in the grass and brush were the sparrow's eggs. Henry never forgot that special moment, and spent much of his life looking at the world and learning how it works.

Compared with the commotion of the Detroit riverfront, the farm in Dearborn seemed a dull place. Henry split wood for the kitchen stove. He helped his father plow the fields. But feeding and watering his father's horses was the task about which Henry grumbled the most, which was exactly why his mother made him do it. If a job was fun, she said, it was not work, and it did not teach a person anything about responsibility.

Henry learned responsibility, but he never learned to make friends with horses the way the other farm boys did. He was different from them in other ways, too. They were interested in sports. Henry was fascinated by machines. His brothers laughed at the way his pockets bulged with bolts, nuts, and flat metal washers. His sister Margaret hid her windup toys from Henry because he took them apart to see how they worked.

Tools were Henry's toys. His father called him a tinkerer. His mother called him "her born mechanic." Being different was a strength, not a weakness, she told Henry. You must find the thing that you do best, she said, and then do it the best you can.

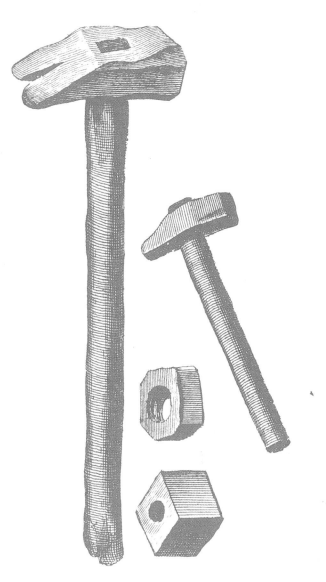

On a Sunday morning after church, Henry discovered something he could do best.

"Albert Hutchings had a big watch chain on his vest," Henry remembered. "I wanted to see it."

The watch had stopped. Henry ground a nail into a screwdriver and pried off the cap. Inside was a mainspring that powered tiny clock wheels. One wheel moved the hour hand. A second wheel moved the minute hand. Piece by piece, springs and wheels, Henry took apart the watch. When he had put it back together, the watch was keeping proper time again.

Soon neighbors were bringing their broken timepieces to Henry. By taking them apart, he learned about springs and levers and mechanical movements. Other boys treasured marbles, but Henry traded marbles for clock wheels. In Detroit he watched a man making files at the Nickleson File Company. At home Henry made his own file. With it he reshaped his mother's knitting needles into tiny screwdrivers. He shaved her corset stays made of bone into tweezers small enough to pinch and remove the watch parts.

Henry had learned an important lesson. Time was a machine that could be taken apart and put back together again.

Above and background: From the McGuffey New Second Eclectic Reader, reprinted by Henry Ford in 1930

THE BIRD'S NEST

If ever I see
on bush or tree,
Young birds in a pretty nest,
I must not, in play,
steal the young birds away,
to grieve their mother's breast.

My mother I know
would sorrow so,
Should I be stolen away
So I'll speak to the birds,
in my softest words,
Nor hurt them in my play.

— McGuffey New Second Eclectic Reader

When Henry was thirteen, he learned the meaning of sorrow and felt the pain of having someone he loved stolen away. On a March night in an upstairs bedroom, Mary Ford gave birth to her eighth child. The baby did not live, nor did Mary regain her strength. Twelve days later, she died.

His mother's death angered Henry. "I felt as if a great wrong had been done to me," he said. More than anyone else, his mother had understood him and expected great things from him. Without her presence and her praise, the farmhouse seemed empty and silent.

"Like a watch without a mainspring," Henry said.

Lonely and brooding, Henry kept to himself for months after his mother's death. Then on a July afternoon, his life changed once again.

He and his father were riding in a horse-drawn wagon when they came upon a noisy contraption crawling along the dirt road. Henry had seen plenty of steam engines before, but they had always been bolted to a factory floor or pulled to a field by horses. This machine was moving forward under its own power.

Henry jumped from the wagon to get a better look. The secret of the locomotion seemed to be the chain that linked the engine to the rear wheels. "How fast does it go?" Henry asked the man who was shoveling coal into the boiler and steering the machine.

"Two hundred turns a minute," the man answered.

The machine gave Henry an idea: The engine's wheels and chain were not so very different from the gears of a watch. One day he would build his own self-propelled machine.

Three years later, when he was sixteen, Henry left the farm and moved to the city. He had taught himself about mechanics by experimenting with watches and farm equipment, but he had much more to learn. The answers to his questions were in the machine shops and factories of Detroit.

A BIOGRAPHY OF HENRY FORD

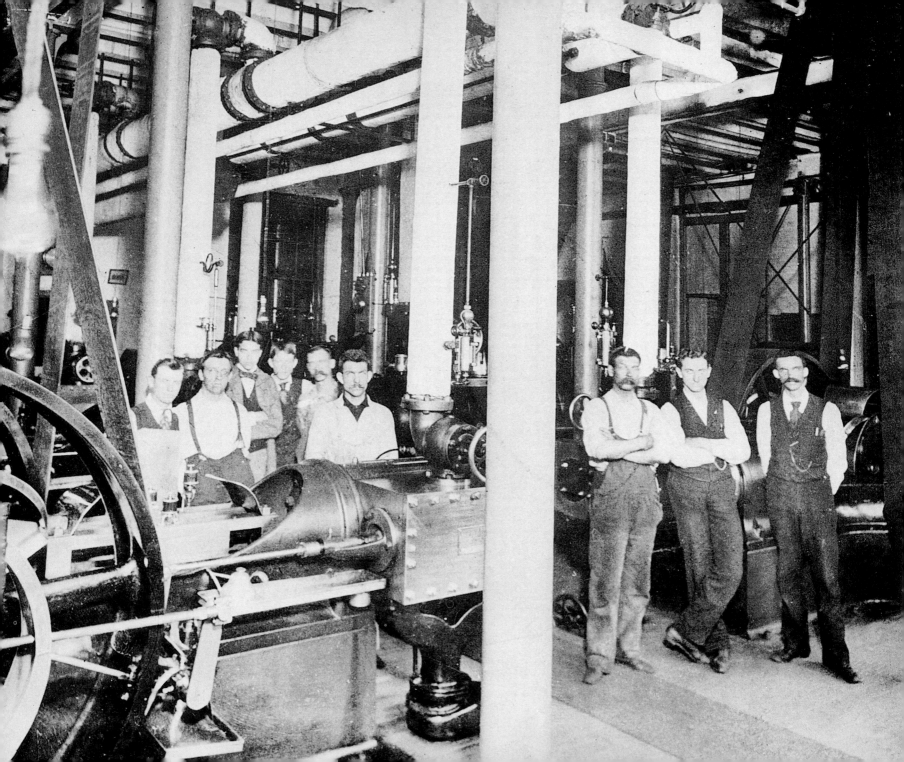

PART II:
RACE AGAINST TIME

*The only way to get happiness is
pursue it. Happiness is in the pursuing.*

—Henry Ford

Twenty years had passed since he had seen his first self-propelled machine. In that time, Henry had built a career for himself in an exciting new industry—electricity. He was a chief engineer for "Station A," the Edison Illuminating Company's main power plant that provided electricity to businesses and homes in Detroit. He supervised the workers who operated the boilers that generated steam to drive the engines and dynamos that created electricity.

At thirty-three, Henry's future looked bright. Not only did he have a good job, but he also had a new family. He had married Clara Bryant in 1888. Their only child, a son named Edsel, was born in 1893. But

Left: Henry Ford at far right in the Edison Illuminating Company engine room

Henry had not given up his dream of building a horseless carriage. In his pockets he still carried screws and nuts and electric coils. The men who worked for him often teased him. "Have you got a piece of an engine in your pocket, Henry?" they laughed.

One person took his ideas about machines seriously—Clara. Henry called his wife "the Believer." Like his mother, Clara expected great things from Henry. Night after night in the brick shed behind their house on Bagley Avenue, he experimented with his newest buggy—a "Quadricycle." The most remarkable thing about the carriage was the gasoline engine mounted behind the seat.

Henry had not lost interest in steam engines. But gasoline engines, which were smaller and simpler to operate, fascinated him, especially if they could be tinkered into powering automobiles. The engine's heart, or mainspring, was a hollow pipe cut into two cylinders. Inside these cylinders, gasoline and air mixed, creating a small explosion that sparked the motor into life. Because the firing occurred inside a cylinder, the engine was called an internal combustion engine.

Clara was the Believer. But one other person fired Henry's determination not to give up his dream. Thomas Edison knew more about electricity than any man in the world. He had invented the electric lightbulb and made dozens of other discoveries, including the phonograph and the motion picture machine. He was Henry Ford's idol. Henry met him for the first time at a business meeting in New York City in 1893.

When Edison learned that Henry Ford was building a gas car, he invited the young man to talk with him. After hearing Ford's ideas, Edison banged his fist upon the table. "Young man, that's the thing," he

Above: Clara Bryant Ford (Henry's wife) and their son, Edsel, in 1894

Right: A re-creation of Henry's Bagley Avenue workshop

cried. "Your car is self-contained, no boiler, no heavy battery, no smoke or steam. Keep at it!"

Henry never forgot those words of encouragement. Years later he would admit that meeting Thomas Edison that day was a turning point in his life.

On a rainy June night in 1896, the Quadricycle was ready for its first test drive. Only then did Henry realize his mistake. He had spent the last three years building the Quadricycle piece by piece inside the shed, and now the car was too large to roll through the doorway. Henry grabbed an ax and knocked down the bricks around the door. Clara heard the crashing and rushed outside. She watched as Henry rolled the Quadricycle from the shed into the rain. He set the choke, spun the flywheel, and the gasoline engine roared to life. Henry and his friend Jim Bishop, who had helped Henry build the machine, climbed aboard and the buggy sputtered away into the dark night.

Henry Ford had built his first automobile.

On an October afternoon in 1901, eight thousand people crowded into the fairgrounds at Grosse Point on Lake Michigan. They had come to see Alexander Winton. Earlier in the year, the carmaker from Cleveland had clocked his race car at an amazing 38 miles (61 kilometers) an hour. Now daredevil Winton was in Detroit to set a new speed record.

Henry had never raced before, but he had long ago recognized the

Above: Thomas Edison in 1892

Below: *The outside of the Bagley Avenue workshop*

Right: *Henry Ford driving the Quadricycle in 1896*

THE HORSELESS CARRIAGE

*It doesn't shy at papers as they
blow along the street.
It cuts no silly capers on the
dashboard with its feet.
It doesn't paw the sod up all
around the hitching post.
It doesn't scare at shadows as
a man would with a ghost.
It doesn't gnaw the manger
and it doesn't waste the hay,
Nor put you into danger
when the band begins to play.*

— Anonymous

importance of speed. If he could build a lightweight car that was faster than any other, then perhaps he could raise enough money to start a new automobile company. Determined to prove himself and the Ford racer he had built, Henry entered the race against Winton.

The starting gun sounded. Winton lurched into the lead. On the curves, Henry cut the engine and coasted slowly, fearful of rolling his racer on the steep banks. After three laps, Winton's 40-horsepower engine left Henry lagging behind in a cloud of dust. The Ford racer lacked power, but its chassis was lighter. On each straightaway, Henry gained speed, closing the gap.

Suddenly, black smoke began to boil from the rear of Winton's car. One of his cylinders was leaking, and the racer was losing power. On the seventh lap, Henry roared past Winton and won the race.

"The people went wild," Clara remembered. The victory proved that Henry Ford knew something about building automobiles, after all.

Speed and fame left Henry hungry for more. He began at once to build an even faster race car, which he named the "999" after a high-speed train. Ten feet (3 meters) long and with four large cylinders, the 999 exploded into life with 70 horsepower. The racer had only one seat, but Henry said that one life was enough to risk.

"The roar of those cylinders at full speed was enough to half kill a man," said Henry. "Going over Niagara Falls would have been a pastime after a ride in the 999."

Alexander Winton agreed to another race. All Henry needed now was a driver willing to risk his life for Henry's fame and fortune. Barney

Oldfield was a successful bicycle racer. Speed thrilled him. Although he had never driven a motor car before, he was willing to give it a try.

On the day of the race, Henry cranked the engine and the cylinders exploded into life. "Well, this chariot may kill me," Barney shouted above the engine's thunder, "but they will say afterward that I was going like hell when she took me over the bank."

Barney did not look back, and he did not coast on the curves. He pressed the pedal to the floor and let the engines go full out.

The 999 was a racing success.

Henry was running out of time. He was almost forty years old. Other men were building and selling automobiles, but the two carmaking companies Henry Ford had started were failures.

One day a friend gave Henry a book called *A Short View of Great Questions.* After reading the book, Henry came to believe in the idea of reincarnation. He was convinced that he had lived and died several times before, and that all his ideas about machines were memories that had passed from his previous lives into his present one. Hadn't his mother called him "her born mechanic?"

Henry had discovered a new understanding of the way things worked. Time was not trapped inside a watch face. Time was not the number of notches on a clock wheel. Time was endless and memory never died. All the great things his mother had expected from him were still to come— if not in this life, then perhaps in his next.

"I was no longer a slave to the hands of the clock," said Henry. "There was time enough to plan and to create."

Preceding page: The first Ford racer, with Henry behind the wheel and Spider Huff on the running board, 1901

Left: *Barney Oldfield driving the 999 racer, 1902*

Above: *Ford (standing) and Oldfield with the 999 racer*

PART III:
TIME AND MOTION

I will build a motor car for the great multitude. It will be large enough for the family, but small enough for the individual to run and care for. It will be constructed of the best materials, by the best men to be hired, after the simplest designs that modern engineering can devise. But it will be so low in price that no man making a good salary will be unable to own one . . . .

— Henry Ford

In 1908 automobiles were only for the wealthy. Other carmakers had not yet discovered a way to manufacture cars cheaply. They doubted Henry Ford and his new Ford Motor Company could, either.

But in a locked room on the top floor of the factory, Henry and his engineers were designing a new model car. Earlier Ford models had been successful. First came the Model A and then the Model B. Those cars were followed by Models C, E, F, K, N, R, and S. The Model N, with a

Left: Clara Ford driving a Model N past the Ford Motor Company's Piquette Avenue plant in 1905

body made of vanadium steel (a lightweight but sturdy metal), was selling very well. But Henry could not leave things alone. He was still a tinkerer. He sketched his new ideas on a blackboard. What if the engine had four cylinders in a single block? What if electrical currents between magnets could spark the engine to life?

Henry brought his mother's old rocking chair from the farmhouse to the locked room and sat for hours as his engineers worked. First they made wooden models of the car parts. Then they worked in metal. Piece by piece the new model came to life.

When at last Henry was satisfied that his car was ready—lightweight but strong, inexpensive but dependable—he unlocked the door. His Model T was finished at last.

Left: Cross section of Ford's Model T

Right: Henry Ford and the Model T, 1921

Following page: Part of the moving assembly line at the Highland Park plant in 1913

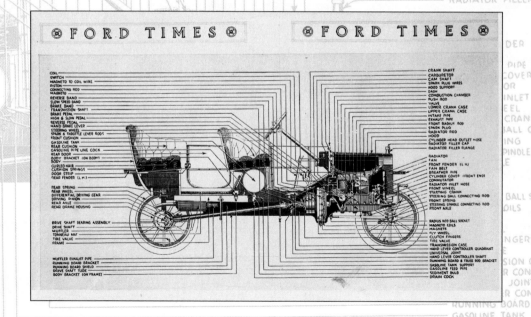

Long ago, Henry had pried off the back of Albert Hutchings's watch to see what was wrong with the moving parts inside. Now Henry peered inside his factory walls. He saw that his workers wasted time whenever they walked across the floor to pick up a car part or bent over to reach for a wrench.

Inside a watch, the mainspring slowly unwound and drove the clock wheels. The hour wheel made one revolution every hour. The minute wheel moved faster, making sixty revolutions every hour. Henry realized that his factory could operate the same way.

"A Ford car contains about five thousand parts, counting screws, nuts, and all," Henry said. He designed a moving assembly line to carry all five thousand parts to the workers in the required order. Some car parts moved on hooks suspended from overhead chains. Other parts moved on a platform.

The speed of the work was carefully timed so that the assembly line did not run too fast or too slow. Where the workers put together the chassis, the line moved 6 feet (2 meters) per minute. Where the workers bolted the front axle to the chassis, the line moved faster, 15 feet (4.5 meters) per minute.

It was like setting the mechanism of a clock.

Henry had created a giant moving timepiece.

Thousands of Model Ts were now rolling off the line every day. By saving time and motion, the Ford assembly line increased production and saved money. Only one thing was wrong with the system. The work was

monotonous. One worker put in a bolt. A little farther down the line, a second worker added a nut. Even farther down the line a third worker tightened the nut. Minute after minute, hour after hour, the workers performed the same repetitive task.

Factory bosses held stopwatches and timed the speed at which the people worked. We must give the workers every second they need to complete a task, said Henry. But, he added, we must not give them one second more.

Henry had accomplished what the other carmakers had not. He had found a way to build a reliable automobile quickly and cheaply. But he had turned people into machine parts in order to do it.

On a visit to the White House to meet President Woodrow Wilson, Henry told a joke about himself:

> An old geezer goes looking for a job. "I'm the guy who used to put part 453 on all cars at the Ford plant."
> "Why did they fire you?"
> "I dropped my monkey wrench and by the time I picked it up, I was 15 cars behind."

In Detroit, the Ford workers weren't laughing. "Which is slave — man or machine?" they asked. Machines were inventions meant to serve society, but inside the Ford Motor Company the machine was the assembly line and it was master.

Bored and exhausted from the dullness of their day, hundreds of workers quit their jobs. Without enough workers, the assembly line was like a stopped watch. No Model Ts rolled off the line. Something had to be done.

Preceding pages:

Page 32: *The Piquette Avenue plant's assembly room for the Model N, 1906*

Page 33: *Testing Models R and S at the Piquette Avenue plant, about 1908*

Background: *A crowd gathers at the Highland Park plant following the announcement of the Five Dollar Day*

More than 15,000 men and women stood in line in the January cold outside the Ford Motor Company in Highland Park. A sign on the gate read NO HIRING.

No one turned away. Some had traveled all night in freezing boxcars. Others had walked for days. They had come to Detroit after reading the headlines in newspapers across the country. Henry Ford was paying his assembly-line workers five dollars for eight hours of work each day.

In 1915 most laborers earned $2.50 for twelve hours of work. Ford's Five Dollar Day was a fortune. Other Detroit carmakers predicted the Ford Motor Company would go broke. At least one newspaper predicted trouble of a different kind. The newspaper was right.

Ford had hired more than six thousand new workers and needed no more. Still, shivering and hungry, crowds pressed against the gates. They heckled and shoved the hired workers who were allowed inside the factory. Finally, after days of disappointment, violence exploded in fistfights and pitched bricks. When the police arrived, they turned fire hoses on the mob. The blasts swept the people off their feet and knocked them back in icy waves.

Henry Ford did not go broke. Instead, his Five Dollar Day had altered the meaning of time once more. The Ford Motor Company was now producing thousands of Model Ts around the clock, as many as eight thousand cars in a single day.

Henry Ford had become one of the richest men in the world.

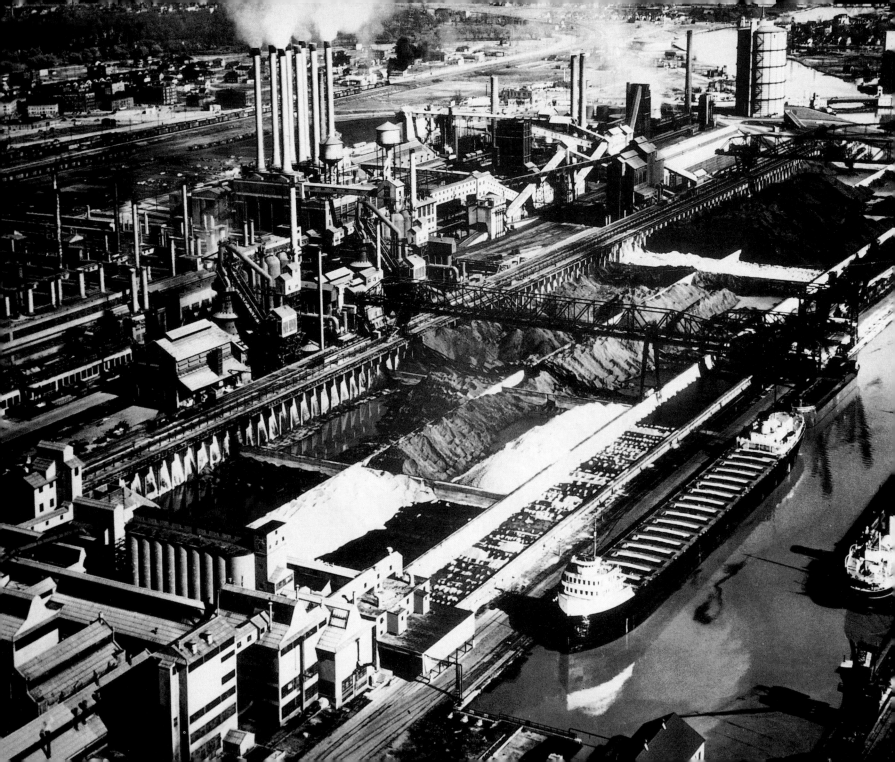

PART IV:
AMERICAN TIMEPIECE

Bob Matson . . . was singing:

> *Ninety years without slumbering*
> *Tick, tock, tick, tock*
> *His life's seconds numbering*
> *Tick, tock, tick, tock*
> *But it stopped short, never to run again*
> *When the old man died.*

Hearing the song, the Boss listened. "Who's that singing?" he asked. The song appealed to him, for clocks and watches were his hobby.

—Irving Bacon, *Reminisces*

Left: The Ford Motor Company's River Rouge plant, 1947

With one foot on the land and one foot in industry, America is safe.

—Henry Ford

Henry learned by looking inside things. Had anyone looked inside Henry's pockets, they would have learned something about him, too. He was one of the world's richest men, but he never carried any money. Instead of metal nuts and bolts, he now held a little black notebook in his pocket. On its blank pages he scribbled ideas he had snatched from the air around him.

"I am going to see that no man comes to know me," Henry once said, but the scratchy writing and the sometimes misspelled words in his black books gave clues.

The way to make more men do a little work is to do more your self.

Henry didn't care much for sitting in his office. He preferred to walk through his factories and talk to his workers. They were building more than automobiles now. Farm tractors, airplanes, and army jeeps were rolling off the line.

More men are killed in one day of WAR than in 10 years on the road.

Henry hated war. His hatred, he said, came from an experience in a previous life. He believed that he had died as a soldier in the Battle of Gettysburg.

What is it the sign of when you sit down on a bee?

Sign of an early spring.

Henry always liked a good joke.

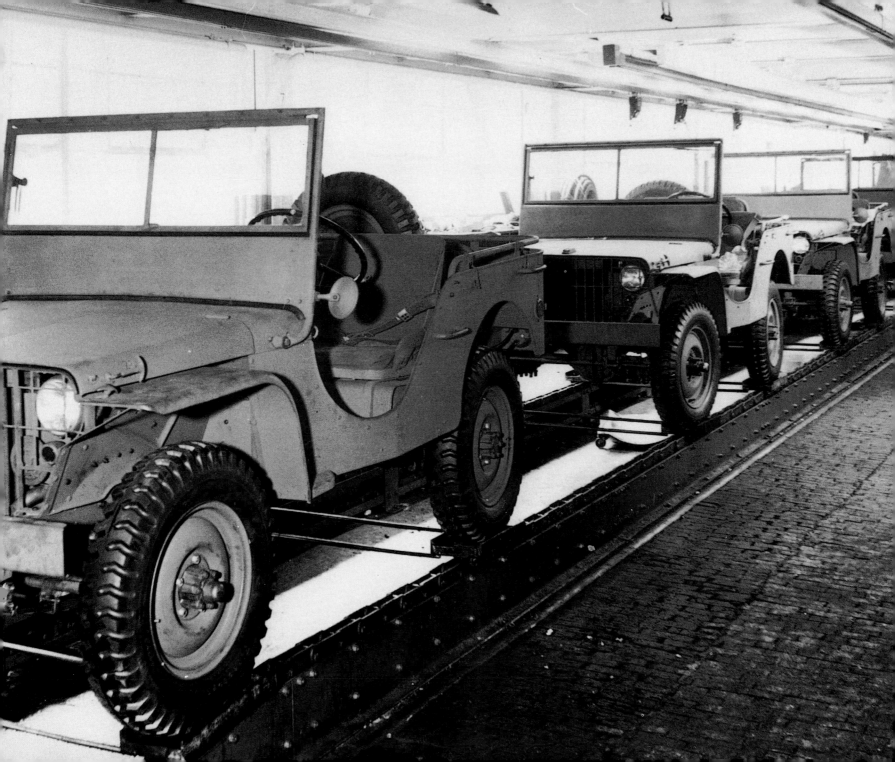

"With One Foot On the Land and One Foot In Industry

America Is Safe" . . . . Henry Ford

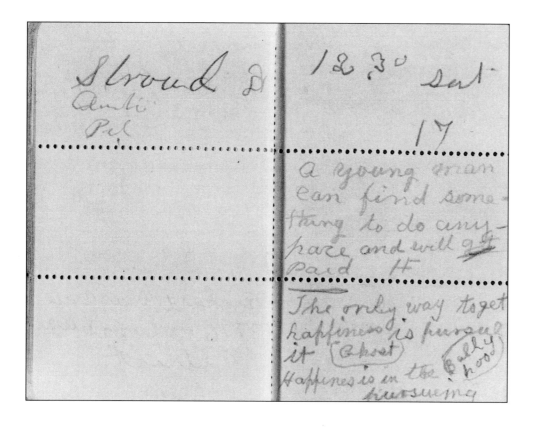

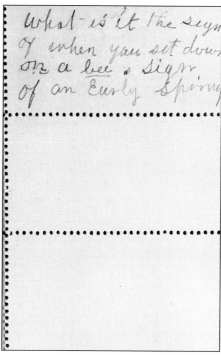

A dirt road had once run past the farmhouse where Henry was born. By 1919 that road was a highway, and the farmhouse was in danger of being torn down. As a boy, Henry had wanted to build the future. Now, at age fifty-six, he began to rebuild the past.

First he moved the farmhouse farther back on the property. Then he began to search for kerosene lamps, old furniture and dishes, even a cast-iron stove, to restore the house to the way he remembered it when his

Preceding page: Ford jeeps on the assembly line

Left: Poster published in the Dearborn Independent, *1928*

Above, left and right: Henry's notebooks

mother had been alive. Henry visited the old farmhouse often. Sometimes he went alone, chopped a little wood for a fire in the parlor stove, and sat in the rocking chair and remembered how life used to be. Other times Henry, Clara, and their friends dressed up in old clothes and went to the farmhouse to dance.

Henry's ideas about time and motion had helped to transform America from a rural country into an industrialized nation. By the 1920s and 1930s, his Ford Motor Company was experimenting with wind tunnels to test new car designs and creating plastics out of soybeans. But Henry was still rebuilding the past. His idea now was to create a museum larger than any other, where people could see how life had been long before machines had changed the land and the people.

Just as once he had saved bits and pieces of metal, he now collected odds and ends of history: potbelly stoves and wooden farm plows, horsedrawn buggies and locomotive engines. He hunted for small things he remembered, like hand tools and children's toy hoops and the McGuffey Readers he had read long ago in a one-room schoolhouse.

He purchased the schoolhouse, too, and other historic buildings— the courthouse where Abraham Lincoln had practiced law and the laboratory where Thomas Edison had invented the lightbulb. He moved entire buildings and their contents, including the restored farmhouse, to an 80-acre (32-hectare) site next to his museum, and called the place Greenfield Village.

The museum and village began as a school where children from kindergarten through twelfth grade could learn as Henry had learned—

Right: An aerial view of the Edison Institute of Technology (now Henry Ford Museum) with Greenfield Village construction in the background, about 1930

by doing. They learned to read from McGuffey Readers. They spun wool on spinning wheels. They tended vegetable gardens and fed and groomed the horses in the barn.

Henry Ford had turned back the clock and gone home. Time is endless, Henry Ford believed, and memory never dies.

Rain had fallen for days that spring of 1947 when Henry was eighty-three years old. On April 7 the Rouge River overflowed its banks and flooded the basement of the Ford home at Fair Lane. The muddy waters cut off all electricity to the house. That night, Henry and Clara ate supper alone by candlelight, the room heated by a fire in the fireplace.

After supper, Henry complained of a headache and went upstairs to bed. A few hours later, alarmed by Henry's troubled sleep, Clara sent one of the servants to bring a doctor.

Henry had been born at a time when candles and oil lamps lit houses, when horses labored as machines, and when unpaved dirt roads led to family farms. That way of life was gone forever, but on that stormy April night, for just a few hours, time seemed to turn backward.

The doctor arrived, but too late. Henry Ford had died by candlelight just before midnight.

Right: Clara and Henry Ford bird-watching at their home, about 1915

BIBLIOGRAPHY

In writing this book, the author relied on archival material from Henry Ford Museum & Greenfield Village, including the Fair Lane Papers, Ford family home movies and moving pictures, and oral histories/reminiscences from Irving Bacon, Oliver Barthel, Faye Beebe, Albert Delorge, Inez Henry, Harold Hicks, Leon Pinkson, Mrs. Stanley Ruddiman, and Charles Voorhees.

Brough, James. *The Ford Dynasty: An American Story*. New York: Doubleday & Co., 1977.

Coggins, Frank W. *Clocks: Construction, Maintenance, and Repair*. Blue Ridge Summit, PA: Tab Books, 1984.

Collier, Peter and David Horowitz. *The Fords: An American Epic*. New York: Summit Books, 1987.

Daniels, Jeff. *The Anatomy of the Car*. London: Brian Todd Publishing House Limited, 1988.

Ford, Henry. *My Life and Work*. New York: Garden City Publishers, 1922.

Garrett, Garet. *The Wild Wheel*. New York: Pantheon Books, 1932.

Gelderman, Carol. *Henry Ford: The Wayward Capitalist*. New York: Dial Press, 1981.

Guest, Edgar A., "Henry Ford Talks About His Mother," *The American Magazine*, July 1923, Vol. 96.

Head, Jeanine M. and William S. Pretzer. *Henry Ford: A Pictorial Biography*. Dearborn, MI: Henry Ford Museum & Greenfield Village, 1990.

Kent, Zachary. *The Story of Henry Ford and the Automobile*. Chicago: Children's Press, 1990.

Lacey, Robert. *Ford: The Men and the Machine*. Boston: Little, Brown and Company, 1986.

McGuffey New Second Eclectic Reader. Cincinnati and New York: Van Antwerp, Bragg, & Co., 1885. Reprinted 1930 by Henry Ford.

ABOUT HENRY FORD MUSEUM & GREENFIELD VILLAGE

Automotive pioneer Henry Ford could afford to purchase great works of art by the truckload but instead chose to collect commonplace items such as toasters, stoves, and farm equipment. When he established the Edison Institute of Technology (now Henry Ford Museum & Greenfield Village) in 1929, his goal was to create a home for his collection that would preserve and honor the history and accomplishments of ordinary Americans.

Today, Henry Ford Museum & Greenfield Village in Dearborn, Michigan, is the most visited indoor-outdoor historical complex in North America, and Michigan's principal cultural attraction, drawing more than one million visitors annually. Collections are housed in the 10-acre museum building and in the 260-plus acres and 81 historic structures of the village. Henry Ford Museum & Greenfield Village is a private, not-for-profit educational institution that is not affiliated with or supported by the Ford Motor Company or the Ford Foundation.

Henry Ford Museum & Greenfield Village
20900 Oakwood Boulevard, P.O. Box 1970
Dearborn, Michigan 48121-1970
(313) 271-1620   (800) 343-1929
http://hfm.umd.umich.edu

ABOUT THE AUTHOR

Catherine Gourley has a passion for American history that comes through in her writing. She is the author of the Millbrook Press's *Hunting Neptune's Giants: True Stories of American Whaling* (in association with Mystic Seaport Museum); *The Courtship of Joanna* (published by Graywolf Press), a historical novel set in the coal country of Pennsylvania where Cathy was born; and several short stories. She is also the author of Millbrook's *Sharks! True Stories and Legends*. Cathy was an English teacher for eleven years and is a former editor of and contributor to *Read* magazine. She recently moved from Connecticut back to her native Pennsylvania, where she now writes full-time.

Cathy's research for *Wheels of Time* took her to Dearborn, Michigan, where she explored the vast collections of Henry Ford Museum & Greenfield Village, and was inspired by America's agricultural past and industrial progress, much as Henry Ford was.